Gathering Grounds

Harriet Tarlo

Gathering Grounds

2011-2019

with images by Judith Tucker

Shearsman Books

Published in the United Kingdom in 2019 by
Shearsman Books
50 Westons Hill Drive
Emersons Green
BRISTOL
BS16 7DF

Shearsman Books Ltd Registered Office
30–31 St. James Place, Mangotsfield, Bristol BS16 9JB
(this address not for correspondence)

www.shearsman.com

ISBN 978-1-84861-669-1

Contents

Tributaries

2011-2014

in place, drawing
where things
start, where to
cut landscape off
seam or folded
    . lead
turning at an
imagined centre, it
begins with a
line in space

(for Judith Tucker)

"Isle of Skye", A635

either side's a ruin *Top o' the Hill*
   Isle of Skye Hotel road-split
     and *a view*, arm on a gatepost
      holes for hinges

   planes out of Manchester
     out of light-dark cloud move over
    curve away
   down valley-time
         grouse ride wind
       over tiny cars, wing
     back to moorland   silver land
        rushes, water
         running out of
       winter ice circling stone
      to summer cottongrass
     patchy featherbed moss
    depleted peatland

   top road sounds like
     water, catches water sound
rolling over slab against slab white water
    between light side
     dark side of valley time

water angles   making pools
unmaking land   what grows
        in and around to
            hold, to funnel
                water

into land: tributaries, slim
        in the crossing
            lengthen
            down their
                gathering
                    grounds

knowing, never knowing their
        flow-ent-end
        into cease still pool
                of reservoir
                collect

even as gas is piped
        through these hills' hearts
            from Northern seas
                to us

October: Austonley as was
(Hoowood Hall, Bingley & Alison Quarry)

                behind blocked gateposts
                        on the rockery steps of a
                garden-not-gone
                                tracing
        walls-through-bracken
                tall seeded nettle
                stalks falling
                back to spread under foot

                        flow
                                line
                                        avenue

                        into flood

                land *taken in*
                        to farm   land
                                               harvested
        stone   into   wall
        tree   into   timber

                        hawberry   dark   fader
                                          heather
                        into
                        quarry
                        pit

KEEP AWAY

drilled millstone grit

plug and feather

listening for the ring

none of this was here

October: Hey Clough to Bilberry Reservoir

sedge   curve   lines
                in and
           encircle darkened
water   origin

valley corner
      rustling through
                    where it is now
                    it was then
      scrub oak white birch
         in dreep heather
         growing low under
            wind

                   white-throated reed
                   bunting shifts
                      along edges

fold water under
      rosebay cloud heads
      foxglove seed pods

                branch ends
                  burying into water
                soft needles
                  slipping into water
                stone cornering
                  down to water

water ever-falling, finding
water

close in louder
and fall
broadening

stream song   against
reservoir silence
being drawn
off

November: Nether Lane, Bradshaw as was

        cows lean up against
                half chimney, fireplace
                        in farm walls pushing
               apart corner protect angled
          lichen soft roof
          arch below

                frost-gold bracken
       rust-metal holding land up
               tree burst out-wall
        light flickering start/stop

                                kestrel's moor colour
                                back over no-mend
                                post & wire cracked
                                stone pragmatics
                                half moon pile

sparse bilberry leaf
holds to plant new
windmills over ghost
field pattern scars

                            clumped green silvered
                            land and water light
                            under foot
                                        broken

                        down white line
                                        fallen wall

                fox head knocker
        on Hunting Lodge door
            PRIVATE: KEEP OUT
                wooden windows see
                        any stir   prey

                                                look there's nothing
                                                there   all those pages
                                                struggle heather stone

                                                land   echo   duck

                nest suspended over water
                        in no leaf branch
                                flight landing
                        bracken under white
            frost   drops
                        melting slight sun
                                water down-run
                                    green stone-pipe-vat-
                                stream-sink-Holme

November: White Walls Lane

scale

            crumpled

                shadow

creas

                ed   dark down

                        side

                          deep

                      ened   in

                gull shoal

            silver-spin   metallic

                on blue   lit

                  and up

        stone sweep

lane

        curve

 through

        and up

        fields

fallen

           farms

              upright lines

            dark darkening

          downward under

            sky-turning

blade-white
wings
    went

       cloud-feather tree-tips
          flare up
        over grey green-lit
        wall-shade, sun-plane

     half moon stone
          bracken leaf
enters   ledge-
         layered

      powder
     lichen green light
      spreading

               cave   low
               in wall, lintel
                  slipping

        red-purpled
       bramble branch
    creeps through stones
spaces, trails before, below

               walled-in water   heard
                   trailing under-hill
            flat fern reed seam wet
                where it went

     to let through-flow
under
     be gathered
trough
     for animals to lap?
     for quarrymen to drink?
     to wash cut stone and slate?
     to form a well where women came
     from farms, jug on that ledge
     in dank green space?

          out into sun
              lone wall posts
          mole hills
             stone heaps
         all-black   against
          high valley
          side
          under-moor

December: Blackpool Bridge

i.m. Dakota people of Bdote/Fort Snelling, Minneapolis, 1862

<pre>
        in
          over-lapped
     snow-curved
                space
     dark-gold
                bdote
     flows

                        down valley-line
                                snow birches
                        grow out
                                white
                        between green

        bracken
stalks
        heather
tops   through
        crystalline
flaw

                        heard water
                        flow freeze flow
</pre>

January: Spring Lane

<pre>
            wall end edge hangs
                        holds
                                from fall
            into
                        reed light
                          space

            weight
                                    wait

ice planes
        cast up
over path
        poised
against frozen
        grass

far path curves
    up to
unseen
        stop   and along
                folded field side
        on side on side

                        plane breaks sky
</pre>

                    moor dreep
               colours
                  flow down
                  silver
                  channels
                  down
                  valley

  smooth black
         light
    falling over
  stone, over
   water
forming
air

               tangle bracken
             silvered orange broken
              each onto   into
                  other

February: Hey Clough

Under alder, under oak
    valley greenside
flat fern orange
    underside under
    foot

                eye blurs – floats –
                      meets white valley
                        icy tributary

                thin fall-sounds
                  water drops
                    wide
                      into
                  water

where to tread
        snow marsh
    snow heather

                  sleet's slow
                    landing into water
                onto ice
                    holds rock
                      islands' summits
        in moving water
                    shadow
                  bends

gripping heather
up to bank
where to tread
where to stand

            deeper in and
               under ledges –
             at the coldest minutes
               of night – water stopped
             into ice, little
               pillars seeming
             to rise

   higher still
each day's melting
   forces waters fall
  on fall on fall
  it flows again
   gritstone
ledge over ledge
  between iced
   limitations,
     edges

              under old bracken's
            broken gold, frozen reeds
             weight-bent over
            land's flecking
             to sound's water
              making space

February: Under Black Hill

inland gulls
white-wheel winter
over almost snows
long held crevice

over rust-wired
stone frame fall
ing farm into wet-light
reeds gold-green

water went wend
ed beck time found
over under place
line

stone corner stand
post path clough
curve low crossing
flo w ent

great gritstone slide
green tongue
land
guide among waters

small white fall catch
-eye in winter-dark
heather under
pale sky

slabbed stone smoothed
sped drop gradient
and turn
is still that same water?

speed sheet gold to white
glass stream speed
into under pool
burst

March: Issues Road

around, above
                        where Issues Road runs out
                each deep white crevice of Black Hill's
cragsides where snow holds form, sets new con-
    tours within old, freezes wind-made drift
                        from falling

                formed

                crystalline edges of delicate weight
        around space, resists hard scape of wall, sheep-
creeps, road, bench, lintel, gate all taken, taken
                    up into incremental shifting
                    shape, just shape

                or meets in snow echo, gate curve
    rising over-drift, capstones patterning out
                        places

                heather tips up ice crust, reeds
dip down lines on white bank
                    by water running green

                        lapwings land drift field
    lift to
                    call through sky

                our set land is not ours

under the play of snow, all falls
                into negative, deep slate reservoir,
dark sheep on darkened fields, green gone,
                    swept up in east wind
        to white wave walls and lanes

        signs point into only white
            gradations of white
                in a white world

March: Wessenden Head Moor to Reap Hill Clough

over   grasslands   pale   in sun
boggy rifts   in and between   ice shadows
stone enclosing   disclosing land
up to white-held tops
down to civil space, caught water
lived-in place

ice-stepping between dark heather
still winter and wait   outcrops
land-flanks in little light,
morning shade   grouse
up against nab circle   and out
shallow beyond our
sky-line

coming round land-corner
into the presence of water
counter-slants against walls
old paths, new paths running
merging
shining veins   lapwing calls
to follow
their own thin falling
lines

or climb, finding a way
up through

                    green clefts – ledges up-land
                       flow ing over
            our finding   our names for
                      grasses, rushes

               ice slabbed gritstone
            in greengold rush-shade
              where we can, where we cannot   see
                   underedge water curling against land
                    small falls into each other
              branches converging –
                         delicate blue lines on a
                 pathfinder map –   crossing on stone
                         hollow dip – waters meet – leaning
                  on grass, balancing to slip, to sink

                slabbed gritstone   tongue over
           tongue curling water overhanging   falls
    shoots angles, making pools in
              ice circles   here, it slaps on stone
                  flats out two ways
                    widening clough
                    out
                         unmaking land

                working round the tip to
                      find a dry place
                          get down to see, lying low
                     below path's curve (2 dogs, 1 walker pass)

myriad grasses above   many gauges of green
girth to hear
wind drawing through reeds and rushes
small falls and seeps of water
grass-shadows, grass
pencil, hand over page
how would it be to stay?

standing again, skitter sideways
leaping   the wrong leg
landing on tussock-shift   wrong-
footing uneven scape

there isn't a way
there isn't a way to go
off-path, counter-path
working up to where
they spring, unseen
their several sources
not anything comes from
one

March: Spring Lane to Blackpool Bridge and up Dean Clough

floaters in white space   fog down all morning
peewit calls overhead
frogspawn between grit stone
slabs laid for quarry tracks
stoat runs into no known space

mole catcher's struggling
shape crossing fields above

gateposts stoned into
walls   rustwired
over the top

black cattle out already
under rain-mist
drift-wind clouding

high tiny windows of old
farms
rush ruins between earth heaps   shelter displaced

dark purple corner above clough
beech gold woodland
remnant

curving down to the bridge   bird voices
becks siding round Reap Hill   converging to
shift names and gradients

at valley bottom   dark banks, flat ferns
            between which   seeing little ahead
                  moving uncertainly   in damp invisibility

                        faint light picks out bright new
                          star moss glint, pools in levelled
                        stones, metal shot shells
                                          two ducks fly up
                                    into mist haze   and gone

            water-path   crossing aslant
                over stones, flung up winter-weed
                              to keep footing   Reap Hill coming
                                    away into water, working around
                                what it gives you
                        gathering above
                  over moor masses
            Wessenden Head, Black Dike, Good Bent
                  to fall edge-over
                              shaley banks, stone stages
                        catching on ledges
                              making pools
                                  still
                        down
                        and iron
                  orange
                              scum of
                  ex-ind
                              acid

flock of little birds lifting-
falling, lifting-falling high up
in gaining light of
white sun-disc in mist

heading back
4 bones, 4 feathers
on a fallen boulder
duck pairs head back up

sun brings out rock edges
water edges   now, it's *scenic*

March: Up Reap Hill

        thrilling bird call
over heather red-tips
        no peak
only a levelling out
        and going on
to high bogland – eye
        drawn to posts
for feeding places, little
        else at height, but
pairs of human uprights
        distant walking
bird pairs arrowing down
        golden plovers
over gold-black bog pools
        flies hovering in
yellow flowering reeds
        what's human?
old grouse butts on hill prow
        sheltering ferns
and lichen grey-flowering
        lifting at edges
not knowing where we were
        going was good

March: Hey Clough

softened colour
low clough   climb
        change
climb   green flow
trees spring cusp

three   bird   song
        beck's meander
ing   mouth
                sun
shadow
            sun
into open water

woodstump   be-
        coming stone
cast over light
water   each
    shining
                slate
        shale
    grit

    flat ferns
fresh-sprung
      under oak
bank slide
      to green reed
edges

march morning
  birches bright
flicker   out   sun
  side   to moss
shadow bank

April: Good Bent End

sighting
highscale
over veering swifts
goosanders nesting in birches
over reservoir
one on ledge above
one on the water

over by Nether Lane
cows at pasture
pipes draining water
to troughs spilling
over

Greaves Head   propped up   not to
enter   doorways blocked

ragged walls, ghost walls
their broken field lines
counter

sheep
following long-laid
trails
seem uncontained

lambs white against
walls
every soft edge
isn't

May: Hey Clough

only now   last year's
bracken down
      below slow-grown spring
     green needles

                flat pale, opening valley floor
                    to eastern light picks
                 out birch-tops up her shadow-steep
                  dim-heathery side

        all colour now in water
      full peat-gold, iron-orange
       over weathered shale

                   cuckoo-clear senses
                    scented ground
                 bee-pull, ladybird stem

       bronze bracken crooks
not yet fiddleheads
         looping the ground
       push up leaf layer
        bark door
            from their spreading
       systems   continuous, ubiquitous
                     in this earth

May: Good Bent End

crashing beck-fall

tumble-stone clough bottom

sound unseen over an edge that

isn't, below soft pine canopy, split trees

still seeding cones

bilberry lanterns deepening

red-pink, shaping

chiming red flash from

black grouse   sent up

over crumbling butts

walls wearing down to

remnants   (corners

not standing)   falling away

from peaks   intermittent towers

scatter stones   ground appearing

to revert to common

forager families long-gone

never nothing quite

ending ever, after

every intervention

protection

above those atmospheric planted

pines bearing their

dead branches

rowans, *raun,* root in high

                                peat-earth, inborn line
                          strong spring saplings

                  light-filtering
            may rain silvers fine grey grasses
                    in rays faint glint
                        taken in to pale lichens
            flowering on stone, crust-clusters touch
                    hold warmth

            patched ash-grey
    heather, burnt re-grown for grouse
            laid out owls' hairy pellets, foxes' bones

                        hummocky stumbling in and
                            out of water, peat-holds,
                                    and almost over
                  heather clump
                    bilberry mound

            sphagnum flanks of
                            green down
                rise to slant
                    down
                        down
                                felled
                    to lay, lie, land on land
                            beats the heart up
                    bracken bearing back
                            vapour trails crossing

into cloud
all that
fallen rain swept down
Black Hill   crashing beck-fall
tumble-stone clough below

echoing
traffic up on Holme Moss
over the tops, invisible cars
sound unseen

May: Spring Lane

        swerve
    lands wing lapwing
scaping moors dreep
    colour   not yet new

                        merging
                winter rushes spring rushes
        out of bog, cotton grass coming in, lowland creep

                                mud ruts onto
                                grooved stones
                                quarry tracks
                                corner peewit
                                calls

                edged space
                green-grown
        all-seeped   wetwall
                stone taken

        hewn
                out   moss
        edged space
                green-grown
        all-seeped   wetwall
                stone taken

long levels
crevice-trails down
Black Hill sides to
valleywaters valleywoods

44

                    wheatear still
          on heather   calligraphic black
                    sweeps her body

                              open space
                    between   beeches
                              cuckoo call
                    Black Hill corner
                              first line of green

June: Spring Lane to Blackpool Bridge

Spring Lane
water flows
with flowers
white through
today June

mothers' wary gaze
 over to calves running
  bumping reedclumps
   tails fly up
      warning calls lapwings
      above quarry nests, whirring
    wings beat wind
 I am disturbance
  here

who chases whom? thin curl curlew's beak
 after lapwing after
  gull
   loud
   over wool-scattered fields
    sheep flee to
     corners

above the butts, new green
on Reap Hill, bilberry bright
  against heather – celandine flash

between cloughs, hearing
water in body beat
stone midpoint, each
edge white
impact

even now, bracken, upright
past unfurled, not allowing
open – yet held

cold for June, light rain
almost not felt, let in
emerging lines flat ferns
midge pricks
unseen
feeling

July: Good Bent End

knowing how to feel
green slide sideways July
swoon
or embracing – or soft –

do the black hearts of speeding cars
beat faster, driving over?

slight, strong,
each grass, each
reed each year
on year of growth
deepening green
as it enters
into earth

rowans' young roughness
falling through fingers

away from the single mind
stilled slab along high edge

gaping peat place
ungreened, faint-scented
over-lapping, crusted
edge over
edge
drips down

when land trips you up,
pulls you in, to fall, so

July: Dean Clough

most too shining
winding
turns
trembling
summer grasses thin
through sun reflect

and cloud
leaning in
low in valley-
time, moss slow-
growing through
silver grass

rimstone
growing edge
until water
curl-curves
gleam over to
fall close, unseen

rowan rough
stirring   streams   out
shading and turning
back   over   lines
leaf-water

water weed tips
          just up
                enough to
        ridge-ripple
light levels in July waters
          swift-drift

water angles   making pools
        unmaking land   what grows
                in and around to
                        hold, to funnel
                                into land

August: Dean Clough

mist

    now lifts

    blue in bracken   darker grasses

           purple crossing green   pink in heather

                    rain drift

              kestrel hanging   hill's horizon

deepening colour, no longer new

             each rowan leaf now part

             of parent tree

                 downstream

             gold-fall slanting

           growing white ridge

             on ridge

              to fallen

           pools and islands

mist falls, lifts, thin rain through fern

             scenting steeply above

               shelter under stone

                  bracken cavern

listen   where
                    wind, water   are pulling   reeds downstream
          catching water back
          over rim, counter to

                                   still to see

                                        pappus   fly
                                                      swallow

                                             wind-water line

August: Issues Road to Hey Clough

hearing, sensing
    crossing water
Hart Hill Dike
    hidden, turning
within high reeds
    high grasses
darker by water

GAS PIPELINE
(Before excavating
    call free
    0800 688588)

issues from rock
    ravine flow
fast down to Hey
    Clough low in
waterland peat
    place inside
meander banks

beneath even
    deep bracken
earth's increments
    build shape
through water's
    course no path

only crossing

    ruined shelter
bridge edge holds
    stones fallen to
water, piece and
    place of water

wall parallel to
    water marking
nothing now, here
    then gone, here
again, then gone
    human maybe

slips, islands, rims
    swirling water white
brims into broad light
    pools, widening now
clear golden orange
    clear almost as a
river, tormentil bright
    on the banks

September: Reap Hill

Light-silvered bracken swathe
dips Reap Hill slopes, lower slopes
where the light takes, where the light
falls over late morning   this time
of year, starting to see land's skeleton
again   green falls away, dries
each grass as it lowers, lies, seeding
summer-end light first touch of earth
of paper faint bone trace all down in
some parallel of eye   up to a
single high rowan horizon waving
bracken ridge, not a line, not a single
line, closer they move against each
other, against sky, changing mid-light
no colour high silhouetted above us
as wind takes the ridge   and sweeps
down to heather green-purple, cloughs
sounding rocks, sounding land, one to
each side, in each open ear   closed
red blood-casing, heard or felt, not seen
little marks turning corners, making
corners   crevices where under
ledge moss, flat ferns are, dark-wet
warmth grows them, light fall rain over
them drawn over, drawn over, not lines
just growing, growing over each other —
in the noise of it all, everything looks like
water

Afterwords:

Prior

At Digley Royd
prior to the reservoir

> a cottage called Clough Top
> which also sold sweets
> Hoowood, among the oldest
> with its quined corners and doorways

Up Gibriding Lane
where it bends to the left

> a row of cottages called Ellis Pond
> a gate up to Green Alders, or Owler's
> mill owner's house built on an old farm

Up Hoowood Lane
the spur of a hill

> Victorian Hoobram, Elizabethan Billy Green:
> doorway of 1664, stone windows never glazed
> wooden shutters to keep out the weather

On the corner

> Greaves Head or Soaper's Place – the scourer's house
> Netherfield, Lower Netherfield, the old farmsteads

And up Nether Lane

> Bartin and Goodbent Lodge
> known as "Better than Expectations"

A little further
back, a road led up to

        Bent Top and Moorside
         perhaps Moorgate, a lintel stone of 1398

Up Shathe Lane
the top road

      Shay Clough known as Toad Hall
        where Owd Toady Broadhead lived

           White Walls, farmstead and cottages
          where Owd Jay wove his own Linsey cloth
         hawked his herbal cures for many ills

where the road
meets Acres Lane

     at the crossroads
       WaterLoo Corner where Dolly at Loo
        refused to move: when they came to demolish
         her cottage, she walked out over the moor
           who knows where

(from "A Walk Round Digley Royd and Bradshaw," manuscript by Ken Haigh)

14 farms

it happened at hay-making time, 1939
the Lord Mayor and councillors drove
up in a Rolls with the news - 9 weeks
later, they were all gone, 50 folk or
more, gone to war, to factory, to mill
all but one drowned in his own well

400 sheep – Gritstones crossed with
Border Leicesters to make a fatter
animal – 20 cows, hens scratching
about, our spuds, turnips, cabbages
 and cauliflowers – 2 working horses

a small herd on pasture, a few acres
set aside for growing oats for us and
the horse, a hay meadow set out in fields
a plough and a sledge for fetching peat
from the high moors, that were it

clear spring water welled-up close to the farm
every field had a name – Woomswell, White Wells, Square Field, Little Field

once it was good land – now it grows ever more sour
you used to be able to look out and see not a wall down

and it was only a dammed up pond when they were done

from Jack Eastwood interview in Holme Valley Examiner *and interviews in* Mosses *and* Clough:
Moor Memories in the Holme Valley Area *ed. Christine Handley and Ian D. Rotherham*

Quiet

You see. I had to go into the mill.
I never wanted to go into the mill.

> Methodists and Primitive Methodists
> we sung at the tops of our voices
> we used to sing "sweet is thy name"
> and do you know, I can hear it now

but we never stopped working, we knew
if we didn't work, there was no pay

we couldn't mend holes at that age
we hadn't learned to mend holes

> rubbing your fingers along, feeling
> the pieces for knots; after a few weeks
> they bled; they said you're becoming
> menders

we'd to knot as well as mend
hundreds and thousands of knots

> we'd ten minutes morning and afternoon
> to go out, play at hide and seek between
> those big bales of wool: we stopped
> so quiet

(from interviews with Grace Hinchcliffe and June Peabody in Eileen Catchell's Tales of the Mills*)*

shadowgroynedipshadowgroynedipshadowgroynedipshadowgroynedipshadow

Humberston Beach and Creek

2013-2014

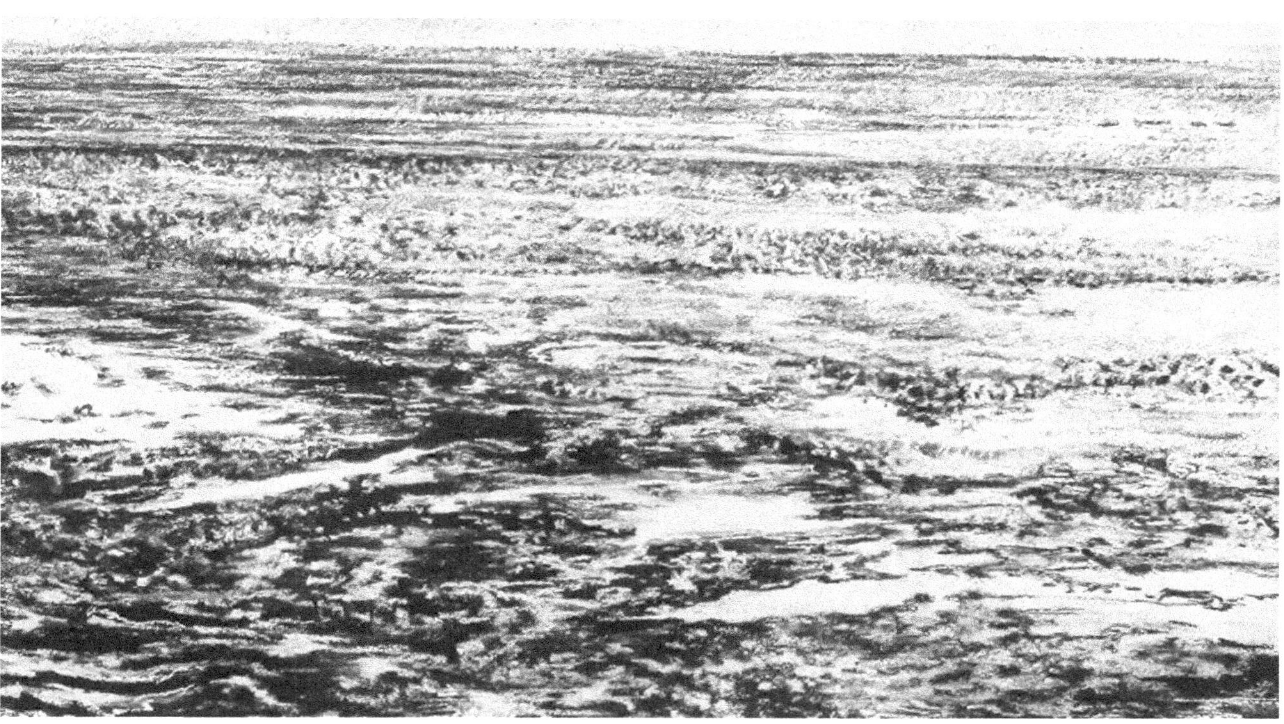

groynedipshadowgroynedipshadowgroynedipshadowgroyne into dune shade

March AM

dark beach streaks:
shadow groyne shadow groyne shadow groyne
and into shade of
pale, pale dune
black silt tide-lines
crows craw
bird-feet deep imprint into
sand moving into mud into sand to mud
clagging, slipping
egret under-streaks
catch white against sky
sounds water-on-shell, wind-
wrinkling runnels and channels
light layering low ridges
scattered spirals, cockles, top-shells
worm-cast bright-edges
small shadow dips

sandpipers wind-rushed running across

still boats beyond oystercatcher edges
awaiting tide

you can get to bits where

DEEP INSHORE CREEK   *all of a sudden*
you can't get back

un-stopping sands blow-build ridges
fill shells open mouths full

ceasing only at green edges
inter-weaving beach to

marsh to soft sandgrass hold
creek-side thick-silted orange to clear-lit green
bubbling beneath mud-cracked
edges dappled grey-pink-mauve and growing

rook lands in an
instant of black

March Eve

       geese cries

              stretch —– join — stretch   out   sky

                           helicopter rips   scatters

               forms again   one single flight direction

   past   dappled half-moon   not yet dusk

                                     gull-wing tense- taut

                               against bitter wind

night-blown   settled snow   stipples sand   layers mud   edges stone

          slows down   confuses   earth-ridges

    dips or rises   unknown points   extend   estuary

May PM

                    smoke grain   pattern   fly
               moment momentarily   alights
                   trails pathways
       grains flight   pattern   smoke
     settling against feet   between teeth   inside eye

               behind sand - water - strand - swerve
  green line of trees   no sign land   behind
     swallows   close   space   between
     still   white   clouds
                           all out into cloud-sand

July PM

stranding

        burying groyne

          closing land

                 raising   thistle

    slip sand   plantain   serrating

          skylark song

  higher than we

     can see

              in green

                out of marsh-mud

          each silver succulent sucks

             saltwater into each

                 soft living leaf

shell salt-mud paths   between pools   through purplegreen marsh

  thrift husk clumps tiny mud cliffs   under high green   all exists

  within bees   skylarks   buntings   songings

                    all things seem floating moored ships   seaward
                          headland   lighthouse   pale   people on
                                                   purple   mud   sand   places

quick quivering horizon
                              every element   growing   distant forts
        as if aflame   or in oil where meets light water colour
masts and folded ship sails shift   shift   shift
                                                        still far edge of marsh

        dark trees above   silvery marram   wind-drift
              grasses dune- making   straggling over
              fence stake|reflections downbank
                                                  shadows
          onto broken mud-sand
              foot-dapplings down
              up down
                          across dry sand
                                into wet colour
                                  lit low into
                                        evening

September AM

cawing, calling

walking in and out   iridescence and feathers
  of the weather   salt glaze-cracked places
dog prints in bubbling mud weed drapes
  reeds up clumps

 moving into shadow   piping, piping over

sandworkings   over the pools, the black dog
   runs, over and in
 into sun
  feathers and iridescence

shell pairs, cockle pairs, cups opening up, open shells their sea

 bird foot arrows, triangle
 over triangles, triples, multiples,
 diamonds of feet

on to fuller creek, light growing golden
 lavender over, inflorescences wash
  out to estuary, wash back
   in to seed in spring

samphire, samphire, pale pink
 tips taking light samphire shadows
  risen all over out of dark-mud flats

                                                                        weed-draped samphire
                    scattered then dense   wet-smoothed dried skin over *cachrys*
            between creeks, stirring pinkgreen, greenpink in low wind
                                                            tasting, scenting salt in samphire
                                                                    shaped samphire

                    casting an eye for figures
            metal detector, cockle-picker, dog-walker
                                            purposes
                                                            the bigger place is sky, so many flights
                                                            and calls   geese knots starlings

                    over fallen wood, sand-filled bark striations, turning silver
                                                    sand gold layered over into each other

            feels like morning   where beach meets marsh   mud-dapple-sand
    creek narrows at curve, where the crossing place is, ripples under wind-line dynamic

                                    crushing tread through   thick softness
                purslane's silver ochres   plantain's purple-greens   no ground visible
                        samphire pink-tipped salt-made succulence plant tangles
            through it all   small pipings fly up and   over warm narrow creeks
                flowing their brown through green through orange gold
                                    mud-waters   full life almost hidden silty opaque
            in shallows, a crab crosses into weed   then gone into camouflage complete

                                    at moments
                            still bubbles hold still

sometimes something flickers intermittent particles shifting surface
rise from below or fall from sky, catching light, seeming
to decide or drift, not one way, but stir
or rock, gentle, within
mud-bowl bank curves
a lapping line of translucent light … follow
and it enters shadow, paled edge, reflects marsh plants
somehow stilled, from their windblown life above, lying over a leaf,
a sycamore wing, a strand of weed   floating   through flickering water-life

long-curved-beaked call of grey plover   urgent over and back and over
marshes, searching mud channels their drying, cracking
slipped sides slow-subsiding
into heaped rich-sludge-thick once-was-water places

as sun sudden behind cloud makes
a new map of wet and dry, mock tundra up above
under it   all feel change from darkened plant to   quietened mammal

but birds shift skies in a second
single flights taking sky-stage one at a time
tern   egret   scoter?

November AM

little low clouds
cloud in pink pale
lit sky

                    tide high up between
                    groynes backed by tight-
                    packed round stone gabions

pink-light up now   catches V of
    sand bank
           going out   delineates
           sky lit between
      cloud brinks   streaming   over wave rims towards us

low sun in turquoise line over horizon up to sudden blue
                              whole sky blue
     nothing dark now but crows' raggedy wings
as tide pulls back from silver white bare sand line   morning
                     the condition of morning

going back in east wind
day, just day now
sea, sky turning
coal-grey
            then silver brown
              night rain drying
                from concrete slipway

                    tide drawing back
              carving up-sweep grooves round
        each stone   baring sand to cold
cloud cold wind   before, around forts
              little kingdoms

                    knot   redshank   sandpiper curlew
long legs
                        branch out over
                              beaks pecking   sudden fast low flights skim away

        and back to
                              sky reflect beach
                                        mud-sand creek

                cloud blown out   over distant line   sun on

                turning windmill   sailing club masts   only all that is high

        quarter rainbow between forts moves slowly up, down and doubles   faint and strong

February AM

     still   from a distance then

bird-lined light morning waters, waders all scales and shades
     black, white, grey   from terns, turnstones, oystercatchers, barnacle geese
    legs rising over their own mirrors, dipping strong necks over their own bills to pull
          writhing creatures out of under low sea

    then bright wind
clouds coming in white on blue
    mud-fast-flow out empty
          us encroaching, approaching into their murmuring

     scatter left and right

   settling at once again   to still/dip/still pattern intent apart together mid-tide   moving out
on sand strand pecking down   to shadow beaks   bodies over-shadows
     on newly uncovered sheen wet spread sandbanks

    shifted beach   surged, swept   in winter storms   from northeast
delicate fencing fallen   stacked   sand packed groynes   half-buried
    sloped up-ways through dunes   dipped down   at bottom   tide in
and after flood   full channels   shells swept up side-on   lodged in sand-mud

    walk on diamond prints-samphire stubs-tiny pink shells-goose shit to
    fullest uncrossable creek pulling its own wet mud-edges in on itself
      filled oystershells orange-bronze sheen
        water's iron gleam dyeing out silver-white

                    shots over away far
                              fall onto
          green-silver-white marsh
                      orange-pink flickers of flowers to come
            old red stena ferry on horizon line
      forts shifting distances flash of slowed colour over sea
clouds run shadows over sand buryings   cover uncover cover

April PM

(for Annabel McCourt)

        appearing, disappearing Humberston

all weather behind, sun-warmth dune, wind offshore blowing hair forward
patterns of water filling and filling   spurn outlined light turns white in water
in warm dunes under jangling wires and sails   sun draws forts closer

single crossings of colour across (red jacket, black dog, stumbling toddler)

           first swallows

thrown-over   weed   wood waste blue rope, orange net
gulls placed selves between waters, weathers   heads facing west
sandcastle forts assemble, dissemble   colours particles corrugation
    buoy   and behind, shadow other fainter salt blue water

Fitties

2013-2019

unwonted animation
mass of driftwood
truly Bohemian
water from the spring
free and easy
reading and walking
wading and gathering

attractive incident
sandhill fires
alfresco meals
summer by summer
the fun of the thing
croquet or tennis
the benefits of outdoor life

from pre-war newspaper reports cited in Alan Dowling's *Humberston Fitties:
the story of a Lincolnshire plotland* (Cleethorpes 2001)
i.m. A.D.

Up North Sea Lane to Fitties

once was, still might be
                saltmarsh
                    low living, low-lying   behind land

dwellings, each   corrugations of   concrete   outdoor chimneys
painted angle   wood brick   shiplack, burlap   leaning on
facing   plane against   almost anything   triangles

                            salt-worn
                    stakes of unclear fencing
                              falling
                  over dry dry land

            marram dunes
               papery pale cases
                 scattered seed-heads
                    distorting
               plastics leaching
               colour among
            buried benches
         facing sandbank
              protection
      from tide's quick creep
        strip over strip of sand
          closing silver-blue on
             purple-brown, already wet

incoming & behind
    just holding
        tree roots
    against wind slanting
        trunks to sky

crows craw
    over
      human paths, counter-paths
      crossing the lines of
        avenue/dune/beach/estuary

            to reach the mouth
            the mouth
            of the sea

Front and Back

front or back where
to post or enter each avenue
tapering to track to pathway
stops at sand or bungalow
blank | fox in window, pigeons
loud at gate, cars lumber edges
midges flicker floaters in & out
of empty plots imagined chalets:
each age its imposition accumulates
pulls down, adds on bricks, windmills
arguments | they lifted it up and
put it down the wrong way round
don't you see, the front should
be at the back

Name Games

Doric
The Hut
The Little Haven
Hideaway

Sunny Days
Happy Days
Come Rest a While
Perfick

Davlins
Petes Joy
Delboy's Den
Janeric

Summer Reign
Sandholme
Shore Cabin
Dun Roamin

Harbour Side
Sunnyside
Peace Haven
Calm Seas

Uncle John's Cabin
Pottering Heights
Crocodile Island
Mandalay

Sea Breeze
Sea Way
Seachelles
Samphire

Bella's House
Ann's Den
Ellie's Place
Eth's Den

Can't do that
Costa Fortune
Double Dutch
Itlldo

The Foxhole
The Willow
Mole Hill Bank
Swallows Nest

Tudor Cottage
The White House
Cherry-Wood Chalet
Le Chateau

Riverdale
Ridgeway
Southover
Rest-a-While

GerryMyra
Marsyd
Kathleen Eric
Berrick's Lodge

Cedar Lodge
Maple lodge
Ash Cottage
Stanwood

Shanty
Creek Cabin
The Pebbles
Cockleshell Cottage

Smogo's Den
Ozzie's Tufts
'acketts 'oose
Smiffy's Cabin

The Flintstones
Fiddly Dee Chalet
Eccentric House
Rise and Shine 109

Love Shack
Teapot Cottage
Ye Old Log Cabin
Cosy Cabin

Kokomo
Nannie and Bampie
Royjunski
Desres

Cape Cod
Melbourne Cottage
Desperado
Wilstelea Bar

The Dunes
Shabby Shack
Summer Den
Waving Marram

Pa Straw's Residence
Graham's Garden
Grandad's House
Kendell's Corner

"In the Doghouse"
Mutts Mansion
Woofers Retreat
The Den of Joy

The Four Winds
Ozone
The Folly
Linga Longa

Evil Eyes
Sea Holme
Era
Invincible

Jolenes
Ida May
Dreams Do Come True
Delphine

Betidyeti
Bee Safe
The B's Knees
Berryhead

The Sea House
The Cara
Estella Maris
Pace et Bene

Belle Isle
Crab Cottage
Chalet Amethyst
Seahorse Chalet

Anchordown
Prospect Place
Endeavour
Neverends

Complements

blue door	red porthole
green window	creosote fencing
beech leaf	marble shingle
pink blinds	pebbledash
white frames	lace nets
concrete crevice	bright marigold
purple sage	silver corrugate
orange brick	pale pampas
cut lawn	resin cherub
quince blossom	bus stop
dull asbestos	repainted red
peeling white	dog roses
sweet peas	long grass
violet cranesbill	bare window
stone faerie	cockleshells
blue stucco	union jack

Do Not Park on the Grass Verge

I do everything myself living by the sea
like playing outdoor house. I came for a bit
and stayed 10 years. I just always wanted
to be on the coast. I don't like being stuck in.
I can't imagine not having it. My wife died,
I drank too much. It was a project.

By the sea all worries wash away

It was the only way to stay close to him
we thought. We needed to be near the sea,
never expected to stay all these years.
I can put colours in I never would
at home. It's the love of my life really.

Welcome   Keep Away

Fallen Fittie

Behind council signs, sumac
heads held on bare stems
through winter into spring
appear edible or poisonous.
Round the back of the flags
strips of unsound wood,
spongy asbestos fallen in
wind or water – once was
holiday – shell jar, bucket,
small crockery stacked in
furniture in miniature china
boy and barrow stood still
on a slim shelf watching

Dunes and Backs

first of **may** apple blossom pink-white in grey-green
morning: dove calls in small rain dripping: wind dropped
tide full up: dying bouquets clung to benches: **LINDA HATES ME**
sandbank dark with waders: water light rolls up
concrete slipway: **currents can easily isolate anyone**
purple lilac bowers over dull green tank: corkscrew willow
bright against red fence: cat's face behind nets

clearouts in early season   **june** piles of window frames
chairs, branches, buckets   priced low or free
a fag on the doorstep
bath robe and towel turban

goldfinch fledgling falls
dog and man race to catch it

low woodland   between chalets
and dunes   back gates push
aside pine cones   under half moon
by gas cylinders   hammock sways
water butts   outside chimneys
so many sparrows   & starlings
through rosehips   hawthorns
high yellow broom   *it really did*
used to be like this **july**

chalets for sale come **september** sprawling with   end of season
russian vine, ivy, honeysuckle turning green stars over pale fencing peeling
colours fade right out in morning light   far ships, containers flattened onto
one false horizon   brent geese and gulls   bicker over catch

bench sunk back in sand   does not see   high rook-chimney
NO THROUGH ROAD]   hips hung red in sparse **november** yellow
apples holding to low branches   **[PEDESTRIAN ACCESS TO BEACH ONLY**
rusting swing angle trampoline   calor gas out back in every shade and fade of blue

december down St Anthony's Bank Road   sense of
back edge   caravans screened   by trees bank
last year's nests   dropping, frosted leaves
below   bitterly but bright   ice puddles cracking up road
pigeon flurry out   from feeder

Fitties close at 4   at road   at lagoon
off field side
yellow jackets set   great geese swirls
barriers to pleasure
drifts
place   grazing
catches wind
february

Turn of Year

swung over   chains   rust round   swing frame   seat long
rotted off   blue sheeting   bricked   onto roof   flapping
    back   over ridge   grows grass   green on the A-line   doors
windows   peeling paint   back to wood   blinds down   gates
    coiled by   dog leads   bike-chains   bungee cords   padlocked
shut   half nets show   a low picture   plastic bird in cage
    plastic plant in pot   endure a lifetime   by armchair   under
alarm   system flicker

    in every garden   a landed   dog/tennis/kids/beach/golf   ball
    in rockery   china cat and hen   face each other
one fresh flower, pink   among fading hydrangeas   over bright lichened
    fence in sun   fuchsias wilt in frost   last years poppies in
next door's flowerbed   concrete wall   stuck with   wine bottles
    glass end circle patterns   glory days   summer parties   under
faded coloured pegs   empty feeders   mini cannon points
    at   pale painted car   handmade at home
    two bench seats and a wheel   no need to frame

Night Fitties

november week-night
dark chalets under dim
lamps glow variegated
plants: silhouettes of
lone lilies illuminate

woman in red top
feeds fox at lit door
frame intimate until
us: lifts bowl, turns
light off, door shuts

t.v. flashes window in
window's wide sight:
big guy in vest jumps
up behind blown rose
flicker white in colour

prow push to shove
fence out, leylandii up
& round long held *for
sale or sold* garden boat
grounded at dusk

hearts hang inside
cold closed summer
houses: few vent
smoke, few gleams
car corners statuary

Fitties Voices 2016

I were 11. Fitties was the first
holiday we ever had. Me dad
wasn't a holiday man but
me mam fetched us. We came
over from Doncaster 60 years
since. We went to see the boats
at Grimsby, played cricket on
the beach here. It were our
first holiday and we loved it

As a little girl, my Dad
down the mines, we came
for Barnsley Feast Week
fetching water from
standpipes, lighting gas
mantles, so careful, trying
not to break them. They
went up from 1 & 9 to
half a crown, up in flames
if you touched them. It was
just mud paths, dreadful
when it rained but
brilliant at the same time.

We came for the whole
Summer from Immingham.
Everyone had a bridge
across the dyke. We'd 8 tin
buckets, we'd to traipse
up and down 3 times a day
to fill em up at the pump.
We'd go cockling, picking
samphire from the beds,
watercress from the dyke,
free-flowing then. Uncle Tom
auctioned fish at Grimsby
Docks; he had about 4
languages. There he is, doing
the roof repairs as usual.

Just after the war, our neighbour
built a bungalow at the Fitties.
It was basic to say the least but
my sister and I loved to be invited
there – it was very close to the
dunes and we lived like gypsies
barefoot and minimal clothes.
We spent hours with the other
children on the dunes and then
came back to devour bread and
jam, fish and chips, then fell asleep
easily on old army camp beds and
dreamed of the beach and sea.

We came every year in the
'50s – my dad built this in '54.
Nothing was here, it was open
to the beach. The cousins and I
we grew up on the sand dunes.
I love the planes going over –
they've always been here. They
flew much lower then, and we
used to wave and they waved
back and everything. We'd go out
to the forts along the boom –
you knew where you were
and how long you had exactly
when the boom was there
till they took it all away.
It's the love of my life really.

Going back 80 years, driving
from Sheffield to visit Grandma
we spent a day here, always
the same: fish and chips in the
carpark, walking round the site
wishing we had a chalet.

When the grandsons were
little, we came for holidays
playing tiddly winks by
candlelight, having a real
fire to poke. We talked of
buying – a pipedream! –
till a card went up in the
window of 182 – "for sale"

I'm a cabinet maker, bit
of all sorts really. A mate
bought a place on 8th Avenue.
I came to help him, never
went home. People kept saying
*when you've done that can you
do me this or can you do me
that?* In two years I'd enough
to buy my own. You bought 'em
from the owners then, you bought
'em as seen, everything in. We knew
it were used in the War, billeted
to soldiers, nothing more. There's
always something you need to do
that you've never done before.

We gutted it and done it all
ourselves, made this garden
from rubble, from nothing.
There's a lot live here full time.
We're all very close round
here. We walk around in our
dressing gowns, help with
building, always a cuppa.
We hut dwellers look after
each other. We took that insult
and used it back. Why destroy
a thing of beauty?

Uncle Len was a trawler skipper
hired a place every year – 8 kids
in 1 bedroom – aunt & uncle &
mother's been here 10 years now
lease ran out years ago – it's
them and us with the council.
The land, Corpus Christie owned
it – then some rich lawyer – now
they don't know – council leased
it, now they've sold it – some
behind the road is owned by
the M.O.D. – there's lots of its
Preservation & Conservation.

It's changed so much,
everyone demanding stuff.
Forty years ago the camp
was like a family feeling
happy. I used to cut
people's grass for them.
The manager lived on site
Rowley Curtis, he'd bring
soil & seed, tapes & poles
to keep people off. Parties,
barbeques, open days
took place at random. I can't
imagine not having it.

I've had it over 50 years this,
about 52. That were potato fields.
At the end of there it were a
tenting field. We used to bring
a tent and put it up and we'd walk
down here to come to the beach.
I fancied one of these. It were
an absolute wreck – half the
roof were missing – but it were
all I could afford. My son did it up –
our Kenny were a handy man –
my husband couldn't do ought.
It's flat here – I can still walk here.
I daren't go up my back garden
at home. There's more foreigners
than English in Dewsbury now.

We lived on the estate
then, no one had cars then.
We used to come up here
with the pram. It was all dunes
around here, all the way to the
old bathing pool. My dad 'ld
come home from work, get
changed, bring sandwiches
up on his bicycle and we'd
have our tea in the dunes.
Them were the days.

My mother's in Cleethorpes
Cemetery – 70 years between
when I first lived here and
when I returned. I didn't want
my mother to be alone. Nothing
had changed. Used to be folk
from Sheffield, all they wanted
was slot machines and such.
They never walked up here.
Down on the beach, you notice it
daily, tides eroding constantly –
we've lost a lot of sand, the creek's
come in a lot. Years ago it was
way out, the dunes were 8 or 10
foot deep. Yep, we've lost a lot

I only come here
when the weather's
good. I've been more
this year than ever
before. My wife's been
poorly, throat cancer
you know. After all
the treatment, the
chemo, we came. My
travelling days are
long gone and the
fresh air helps her
to breathe easier.

When she retired, she didn't
have a lot of dosh, I said to her
Why don't you go on the Fitties?
Her brother was agin it, thought
his daft sister was being even
more daft than usual. People
either get it or they don't get it.
In the end, he got it. My mother,
where she came from, she
wouldn't tell people I lived here.
The words wouldn't come out
of her mouth. But I think it's
within us, what makes us want
to come to the sea. It's primal,
really primal.

I retired at 52, I was bored at work –
ended up an executive manager.
Started life down the pit at 14.
I was there 10 year & 5 people got
killed. They thought they were safe.
No one's safe. All this stuff's here's
what people are throwing away
flowers and everything. Even the
footballer, he was on the tip. You know
the walk to Tetney, I've just fetched all
that stone from there. They call me the
scavenger, and they're right. People think
you've got a screw loose, but I don't care.

This were army barracks. I just took
the army bunk beds out & moved in.
This one's got 3 roofs on it – used
to be a flat roof, then somebody put
a sloping roof on it, then somebody
put another sloping roof on it in their
wisdom. It never leaks to be fair.
There's badgers come here, there's
birds in the roof – we leave them
there – they were here before us.

It's an all-in-one chalet,
my mum's chalet, my retreat
now, probably the cause of the
divorce. We were about six
huge pyracanthus in the garden,
wooden steps up to the shop,
we all used to drop our money
under those steps. I don't like
being in a house. So peaceful
here, the wildlife's all here
frogs and foxes and birds.

come on Dickie, good feller
he just likes the gate open
so he can meet and greet
people – he doesn't like
being shut in – he just
goes in a circle – he
never runs away

Humberston to Tetney Lock

2013-2019

out from Tetney   LAND ONLY

stand alone gate   fencing fallen

tall reeds teasels   bent to water

steel grey canal   push ripple wind

starling packs   turning, searching

field side   over midden

larks, wind   insistent calling

oil pipe loop over   at path's turn in

geese flights go   out to the mouth

7-8 March 2013

(for Linda Ingham)

sun   penumbra   mist

high path through sky
between
field-side, marsh-side
moles up-earthing
shell-laced soil from
under

oystercatchers, ducks, geese
call over – egret white
in wetland

still windmills
I have not ever seen
one move

only birds cross over
and seed:
teasel, good king henry
taken warm root in
field-margin, ochre marsh
silver-brown, salt-rich

                    stone embrasures small   waterside winter purples
                     protections, growing   elder and alder
                    grass, gold-grey lichens   old low hawthorn tight
                                                                  yellow-green tips
                      on mist-edges, forts   in red-pink leaf-bud
                 at sea, oil tanks float out   last year's berries softening
                       over-land   in to their own skins
                 quiet in mist quieter   catkins and cones hanging
                      river reaching   over   sky-side
                   always reaching   falling, some to land
                 sea   some to water

                              early to hear skylarks
                              singing over Tetney
                              what we hear is there
                              but cannot see
                              have never yet seen

22 March 2013

                                                            under east wind
                       straight   raised   place   made   through
      drained land

house   tree   pylon   tank   tree   house   windmill   horizon

under east wind sweep   between low trees   low fence lines   breaking flat flow
            wind ridged water   elder dip dredge   over brown-silver channels   counter
      to canal, draining   tilled pink fields   slow-draining down   through   salt-sand ground
                        but not away from   no-bird field
                                                        hideaway day
            curved block
                        corner
                        along reed, teasel
                                dry blown edge
                                        land meet water

dying branch creak wind
      breaking alder against
        elder's bright lichened
            spike-budded limbs
              hawthorn dark-knot
              nest
            places all along
          cold cold edge
      held still against
    pale waiting sky
gulls
     below, below
       dipping

line   path canal   line   path
          masked sun day

24 May 2013

                    wind brings first evening
                        light out of egret-sky

cow parsley moving   under still windmill
    frame around   oil tanks float paler
concrete embrasure   green in hedge-dark

unseen may singing
    wind slanting sunlit mustard

                            along field ditches
                                        reaching out
                                hawthorn branches
        over silt silver
            drained off

5 July 2013

                                                                    under
                                                        swallows' wings
                    grassland verges grown into many
                                              bendings, singings
            each over other   vetch purples   clover whites
threadings, tanglings through

up from
salt-sand
ground
            quiet estuary   shimmer shadow   people   dogs   bikes   appear
                at path's horizon   grow slow in sun
                                                        wartime lookouts
                                                        viewing purple marsh

            blank dark windows   square centre
            look in to no one   no defence

            look out of shadow   onto meadow
            cattle in sunlight   grazing

still windmill   house   tree   oil tank   house   steeple   oak   midden
        acres of low low crops   paint green   sense of settlement

gate grown open   briar rose open white
        elder wide open   more white than green
                sky breaks open   more blue than cloud
                        crops take flower   take colour

        into midsummer

27 September 2013

walking out
on thin footworn
line
windmills unmoving
elderberries above

egret flash below
white against red
debris …. marsh-
muted orange
pinks greens grasses
windswept in great
swooshes

hawthorn dark
early autumn ploughed
and ploughing earth turn
tractor
dust spray sun catch
light

clumps of tufted vetch
along banks between
marsh and path, field
and path, growing
higher than higher
tendril to stem, tendril
to stem of themselves
each other clinging up
into purple-dark-green
mass slipping into light
or dark, black or white,
as sun's shadows turn in
and out of cloud

out of pillbox three
leaning on lichen
warm grey on grey
watching undefended
England, marsh to bay

beyond oil pipe, beyond outfall
   turn out into marsh tangle   Sand Haile Flats stretching beyond
      set out for elder horizon, haven
          making a quest in landscape

low red clover path   side-angle to open
        red-rusted   gate

   where canal met river mouth
     ships came in to haven
       landing coal and timber
         exporting corn and wool

           now only oil piping in
         from still ship out on the water

Tetney-Haven, at the outfall of the Louth navigation;
has there an inn, coal wharves, and a coastguard station (1870)

along deep cut channel
   marsh creeks, drains, carve
     crevices into mud banks

                          DANGER

                           DEEP

                           MUD

                               scoter flies up and over

                                     heron stands over water

                                         redshanks probing mudbanks

           mud breaks back into marsh in sweep swathe,

                 into its own shining smelling shape

                    birdfoot-patterned   would not take

                                   human weight

old pipe leaking, unknown wood and iron

               workings and winches breaking down

                    to the ground, sinking to join

                        all marsh, every plant

               mud-drenched to the hilt here one time or other

reed rustle knock hollow stem seed   changeable, unsure

               of uneven slippery grass

      bank, its depth

                   far out, a single elder seeded and grown so green

                       above all horizon, haven, silt-rich berries

                              plucked by birds passing

                                almost an edge, but not that

                            more a curve of grassland

                            out into marshland

         no end   slow sea stages of cargo blue, orange, blue block

            hides Spurn Head   now far, now near   depths and distances

                  passing   container   colour

7 February 2014

wind
      merging   turning, verging
         to merge on wing   tear down over
            teasel edges   take direction
            snake back
        separate
          verge merge again
         whirring wings
     over locked
   water
to opened estuary

canada geese landing dark drift on green
    graze sound slow   move over   fields   hundreds as one

9 November 2017

on flood bank
blackbird nest weaves still
hang in hawthorns
from summer

eerie, it *looks* silent   10 turning windmills
whirring like quiet aircraft over
tractor engine turning over
starlings whisking wings

egret lands in light almost translucent
marsh thin dark beak picking over

where surge washed
over, healed greened path

ducks up   from
planks, fish crates

under oil pipe
mustard lichen patches   against darkened red
of gate
out by high wide water   loud gulls, turnstones call

a concentration on movement, on not falling
between two high green sides
little plane passing back & over, over
and back

left of the bank   gathering grounds, drawn down
by colour   plastic bottle tops, blue red green
turquoise dummy, yellow brush

in spattering rain, under oystercatcher high calls

catching curve in
mud-soaked grass
matted reeds of
BULL BRAND universal
refills ULTRA CLEAN
Almost ZERO impurities
crab bodies by
HARROGATE SPRING
rusted tyre in seepy
debris of seeds rushes
reeds TODAYS MILK
WHOLE MILK bleach
bottle pram wheels grown
through Lucozade Energy
pressurised can of
Topping Aerosol Cream
Decorative topping based
on skimmed milk and
vegetable fat UHT Sterilized
Premiere MEGA FOAM
New Formulation HAND &
GUN GRADE IN 1 CAN
THE PROFESSIONALS FOAM
sticking up gun in red
yellow, black rusting
into orange brown
intricate patterning
contour lines of a map
By Appointment To
Her Majesty The Queen
Lubricant Blenders and Paint
Supplies Witham Oil and Paint

Ltd, Lincoln **Qualube**
THE QUALITY LUBRICANT
Lithium EP2 Grease
blue on white flaking
fading, flocking away
in feathers, seaweed stems
pink ribbon wreathing
deflated helium balloon
design fading OUT

rounding the end   marsh golden   fort appearing disappearing   in the gap
   behind   windmills group and re-group in all permutations   112141
      ahead   birds flurry about elderberry outpost   last berries

shift scent from grass   to mud   wrinkled seaweed   stretched out
         on stalks   tautening to   scraps of black plastic
shot gun pellets   blackened stones   in shooting butts

         the moment of channel end   mud tapers out into water   tumbled, marked
            by rocks & shells   browns, creams, russets, yellows   washed, re-washed
            faint faraway Spurn Point   running out to sea
               faint far windmills turning   out to sea   light catches
               single boats   anchors unseen or sensed   moored
                     floated   moored   on estuary

29 March 2019

behind two reflective men ROBOCUT rolls crushing
grass, tin, glass, plants, shells slow over flood bank
to first gate no hawthorn, no alder, no birdsong but
far inland over canal, fields, trees to Tetney
shrunk beneath
windmills

or down on marsh in & out
of ochre   egrets fly land
fly over gold-brown pools, matted
gold-grass fallen swirls   white
wings picking up first flicker flowers
of scurvy grass

shorn path cut banks all way to
oil pipe turn   stumps and chips
stumps and chips   no making
of nest homes, weaving or woven
past & present gone save
a dandelion, little clump
of vetch returning

red glove on rusted gate, hand done
soapy water
fast flows into channel bubbling out
to sea

out to no-elder horizon, no haven
            branches laid out, yellow-lichen living
            still corpse beside its 8 sawn stems

                you could see that tree, hear it, from everywhere

            oystercatchers, geese, knots fly up & on
pushed out as we pass by concrete bridges
                over sea lavender un-flowering
                    rusted gas cooker, faded balls
            laid out marsh into mud, samphire stubs
                salt steaks, yellow oil can
                        scattered rocks
                            to loud honking mouth of estuary
                                final red warning post
                                    at the tapering out

Outfalls

2013-2018

CANAL

cut banks out
water capture
course land
capture course
water Lud let
in let out low
line landcut
line strip sky
seaward but
back-locked
brick-sealed
sluice-levelled
iron & wood
weir & gate
syphon intake
becks & dykes
& drains let
all that wide
fenland Great
Eau fall pipe
pump seep
slack leak in
culvert outfall
channel cut
banks stream
millrace fish-
pond reservoir

intake abstract
flow keep canal-
ised keep flow
(redundant)
against flood

LOUTH

rat jumps in
to black water
& gone under
ragwort yell-
ow edge brick-
yard warehouse
windows broke
long [grain wool
flour] gone
willow-side opp-
oses new brick
housing paved
neat to brink

fast-falling sun-
water old top
lock over, now
tilting weir stilled
on far side bubb-
led slow-green
july enclosure
hemlock lean
morning glory
nettle, bramble
balsam bending
down dark canal
backs banks slips

KEDDINGTON

red admirals
flutter buddleia
to balsam july
under ivied
sycamores let
only little light
paths & pools
flicker in water
checker football
softening since

cracked cop-
ing stone held
heavy up by
brick & wire
empty where
gates hung but

still canalised
streams ever
over growing
edge aslanted
dead-dropped
branches into
falling white
& dark, over
again deeper
ledge deep

LUD

river ruptures out
sluice running Lud
under **DUCKERING
LINCO** iron foot-
bridge worn ropes
hang **JONO ♥ JODI**
twist back jump
turn to cross felled
trunks onto dark
intricate paths in &
out of bushes from
town where they
brought each other
down here down

clagged over ditch
under hedgerow
brushing mallow
bedstraw clover
whites
          & flows
again into plantain
sorrel meadow **DR
PEPPER & PEPSI**
caught at reed
cress edge, winds
to roadside behind

greened barbwire
creep-ripples to
small stone bridge
wanders north-
east into fen

TICKLEPENNY

bramble brick lock
curve purple dead-
nettle haw & ivy
hanging over tumb-
ling white into
pale-aged orange
rounding echoes
on land's quiet
side : thrush lands,
sings on july elder
all green berries
not yet turning :
on Eastfield Road
cars run louder
in parallel dusk

a little clip off
early moon nov-
ember never now
to level out to stop
fast fall down to
rosebay-choked
lock chamber be-
neath concrete
bridge off Cowslip
Lane : blackbirds
sing-fly from aged

hawthorn to still
scraper arm of big
yellow digger on
green near dusk

FARM

alongside thistle-
lined arable River
Farm bales new
piled hay: crop
scent succumbs
to sweet bastard
balsam : swallow
pair cross canal
imposter, grassy
land tongue, river
over hedgerow to
road re-places all

COWS
CALVES
AND
A BULL
GRAZING IN
THIS FIELD

small whites flit
wild meadow-
sweet edge to
rape escape :
screened sewer
age works drain
effluent out by

willows: single
swan & reflection
slow swim head
dipping legs up
stretching & on

ALVINGHAM

weather vane
atop brick barn
once Ship Inn
now Lock Farm
sees northeast
to turbines high
over fen farm
pylon tree cast
white air into
weather : sees
south along
water lines to
Louth's filigree
steeple : half-
grown ducklings
trail a line hid-
ing in verges &
out again : weed-
green Lud drags
downstream still
filters under to
mill pond race
wheel, then back
by Westfield drain
& gravity : lock lies
low, bubbles under
imagined gates

grows bright stone-
crop where goods
wharf was

HIGH BRIDGE

three quarter
november pale
moon: brick base
of wood swing
bridge merges
into concrete
parapet direct
reflect on mirror
sky strip lane
navigation takes
northern turn
narrows between
teasel blackthorn
tangle bank small
half-buried plaque

**In Memory Of
PEARL IRENE SIMPSON
1943-2013
A Wandering Star**

clouds shift pink
afternoon sun
falls on farside
over swan feather
edge, gold spread
sycamore on water

on damp-mown
land : reed warblers
& wrens heard
not seen settle to
hedges & verges
white egret wings
over darkening
canal float back
last cloud light

TOWPATH

cows amble-graze
above : shove at low
tow level, rape stalks
to shoulder : pappus-
webbed thistles clump-
ing bee-clustered
orange-purple honey
& bumble feeding
crop sprayers draw
water off, whirr over
something catching
at eyes, throat

bikers flash over
Fire Beacon Bridge
on july spin : kingfisher
darts blue beneath
onto kingcup yellow

canal narrows in
burrowed banks
[water vole /rat?]
pumping stations
cross, pipe & syphon
in & out of treatment
works, walled reservoir,
swan sits low on eggs

high above her land
rises to western wolds
where Waithe & Lud
first stream up

WAREHOUSE

dragonflies flit over
mown grass curves
bulrush still pool
by 3 stories 7-bays
iron staples holding
walls in, bricked-up
windows, pigeon loft
up top **T.H. 1821** :
steel gantry raking
debris towers high
over stone wharf
winch wheels scour
timber : Old Fleet,
Black Leg drain in

drive up on 1031 at
Thoresby, park, unload
sit up high at fish retreat
cast your lines catch
far echo shots, clay
pigeon drops : call of
gulls peewits geese
flying up over & back
to farmland : poultry
stink from sheds over
bridge : buntings rise
sink rise in rushes till
red-gold reeds low sun
slant line canal-side

NEW DELIGHTS

low where horses
trekked yarrow
nettle thistle trail
pale to darkest pink
july through high
wind-lit part-purpled
teasel, silver-green
bracts & spines, Tetney
church tower sways
behind deep willow-
hidden wells : buzzard
circle-soars over high
yellow ragwort down
low to watermint

red tractor & baler
send dust flying, larks
high over windmill
turn, oil tanks' green
on green : starlings up
over gates & hedges
telegraph poles hay-
wire lines & high
pressure pipeline
warning posts bright
white & orange stalking
over farms & cross canal
from Theddelthorpe
to Killingholme

TETNEY LOCK

november wrens
& redwings feed
on bright rosehips
up through haws
angle error teasel
DANGER OVERHEAD
always carry rods
level, parallel to
the ground walk-
ing dead & alive
grass trod up by
hooves & moles

rust-red farm
bridge girders
spider-woven
MAX 3 TONNES
fisherman sits
behind his line
texting intent

cars strip silver
around away on
North Coates Rd
moorhens take
long canal curve
left : shadows slow
swerve on water
cattle across drink

call deeply chime
to unseen machine
scrape : grey heron
flies far upstream

TETNEY HAVEN

out past oil pipe
out past sluice gate
saline protection
Sand Haile Flats
stretch, samphire
awaits may : red-
rust gate side-angle
open : canal outfall
merge Lud mouth :
here ships exported
wool & corn, landed
coal & timber

DANGER
DEEP
MUD

reed rustle knock
hollow stem slippery
red clover path by
deep cut channel
creeks crevicing into
marsh : scoter flies
up & over grey
november : redshanks
probe mud swathing
into its own shining
smelling shape not
taking human weight

TENDER SUBMISSION

economic engine eco-
logical compensation
flows primary drainage
channel reverting back
to a more semi-natural
ecosystem conservation
designated assets with
historical value access
amenity recreation

now abandoned

un-navigable

wildlife corridor

fish passes

new marina

heritage trail

tourism

healthy living

social inclusion

employment

restoration

diversification

Past Winters' Sonnets

2017-2018

Tetney Lock Bridge

Whiling time, waiting wharfside for tide to
force gates at Lock long gone, across from
brickworks and claypits become caravans &
fisheries, took a beer at the Crown and Anchor
or Sloop Inn, a house among houses now
like Chapel and Coastguard Station – all cluster
along a triangle of lanes & waterways. At the apex
Navigation & Mother Drain merge to fall through
tilting weir from sluice to outfall sluice – exclude
escluse salt from fresh – turnstone flies over flood
gates, under pipe siphoning sweet oil from sea line,
then out & out all gathered rivers, becks & drains
under winter-flocking geese, swirling starlings
through whimbrel marshes into wide tide mouth.

Fen Bridge

Here bees farm hives: chew, store, seal, comb,
clean, seem safe in still garden space behind
great shuttered warehouse at Austen Fen
Poulton Tunnel & pumping stations east
and west keep draining, siphoning – here's
honey and water, water and honey. Suddenly
certainly on far side of bronze water, a horse
rides along Treasure Lane, precarious in power
pole & cable frame before bucolic backdrop
of hay-rolled gold on green. Hunt value here:
white honey, yellow wagtail on Bridge Farm roof,
finches feeding by Fen Farm Cottages. King Lane
to Fen cuts fast through it all on a blind lateral over
the water past Anka, Amaryllis, Bienvenue.

Firebeacon Bridge

Terminus, then coal port. After the Ship Inn fell
into the water, new built bungalow & boatyard on
Bull Bank leading to reservoir, high walls exclude
over farm & marshland. Canal path widens above
nettle patches of wrens, badger pathways
between shining thistle rosettes, vole burrows
into bankside loam, reedbeds below. From far,
gaining ground, bright yellow digger on caterpillar
tyres black scraping arm thrashing out into water
back-drags cracking reeds & plants up onto side
a grubbed-out season's growth dumped, scattered
with scallops & winkles. Something does happen
here: no creatures seen to scuttle but they do:
shaved space made, clear flow maintained.

Out Fen Lock

low amongst grasses under blackbird
calls, bird-scarer shots, hear Out Fen's
full-fall ahead, loud as road where no
road goes. Straight iron cylinder in rotting
wooden frame, east wall standing, west
fallen water outfalls gold white edges
against green-grey before the slight bend
ahead then long straight stretch the stress
and pull of Towing Path to Austen Fen,
then Fire Beacon. Across starlings flock
along banks crossing low and massive sun
ball's dusk throws last purpling light over
the water onto windmills cold turning,
backs of feeding sheep beneath.

Church Foot Bridge, Alvingham

Wagtails call on wing low by winter crops
kingfisher darts turquoise upstream. Behind
the farm, cows pasture over earthworks
priory moats & banks, ditches & fishponds
PUT ON THE WHOLE ARMOUR OF GOD
Let the wealthy give land and alms so *our*
meadow and all the village of Alvingham
next to the dyke in the east are protected
from flooding – till the plague took them
THE ETERNAL GOD IS THY REFUGE
Chasing a trapped wren round St Mary's
damp white spaces, held by anxious corbel
heads, dark green lichen growing over font
Underneath Are The Everlasting Arms

Keddington Church Foot Bridge (Eastfield)

What's behind fences, gates creaking open
into other sides, properties chosen privacy
over view. Just off the towpath, the Raven
beerhouse and bit of land out back, long
since private: cabin and chair look onto
canal's past thirsty workspace, diminutive
drink left out. Blackbird goes blithe between
gardens gathering, flies over roof to drink
at rainwater-filled *Deep Excavations* – diggers
on Eastfield Road *WHERE TOWN MEETS
COUNTRY* – takes low flight back over frost-
laid grass swathes and off down canal kink.
Even in December you could never write
the ground or the growing growings in it.

Tilting Gate Foot Bridge, Riverhead

From brambled banks of split concrete
gulls call through unseen traffic behind
Woolpack, warehouse, mill. Ducks hold
heads low, face east wind on rippling canal,
outfall pipe spouts in. Stacked breeze blocks
at the builders' yard before sun-streaked
factory facade **U.K.** picked out, light bricks
against dark, where goods were hoisted out
of shuttered doors & windows miniature
over the water. The old geezers head along
the wharf past shades of granaries, kilns &
bone mills into the Gas Lamp. Nettles weaken
on the bank, leaves at every stage from
skeletal to new-fallen. *Are you cold there?*

Louth Stories

2016-2018

LUD

She springs up near Maidenwell and up near Cadwell – those are her sources. Welton Beck flows in too, near Thorpe Hall – it all links in. She was diverted from North side to Thames side (tamesa, Celtic for river), a new cut run under Luda Terrace, where the tunnel opened up to the sluices so the old rivers, springs and streams could top the canal up, keep boats sailing, stop the need to pay for towing horses. They said in the 1750s that the amount of water came down from the Ludd could fill the canal every day. That all changed in the '60s. They needed more water for the reservoir at Covenham and the Humber factories – some of them had their own boreholes but they were lowering the aquifer. They diverted it again from Commercial Road across the road to where the housing estate is now, they dug a cut which is Thames Street – it now comes straight out at the canal head. They fed a pipeline in from the Great Eau at Theddlethorpe. Before then the Lud meandered on the North Bank, she still had her main tributaries to Grainthorpe Haven and Somercotes Haven. It was all pushed up North.

Riverhead

When the boy was about 10 he went down to the Riverhead to the U.K. building where Uncle Tom Coggle worked in the coking plant, took an old pram for a free load for his gran. The pram came from the Top Lock – people threw all in there and the lads pulled all sorts out, old axles and the like, to make carts and trolleys. He watched the huge ovens where the coal burned and got pushed out by the rams at the back as coke till North Sea Gas put paid to it in the '70s. Years later the teacher realised you could teach all history from the Ice Age to the present day from one out-of-the-way town. The real obsession now though is the boats – the keels, sloops, ketchers, billy boys and schooners. *When I'm cremated my family knows they're to take my ashes down to the Riverhead and dump 'em in the canal where I've worked, researched, even been down there in a little canoe – had to lift the damn thing up and carry it round the locks mind. Toss 'em in the canal – some would stay there, some would go out to the Humber, to the North Sea.*

Canal and Offshore Marriage

She grew up at the sub-post-office on Newmarket her dad was the best known man, best known shop owner in town. Nana lived in a bungalow on Eastfield Road behind the gas works that backed onto the canal. Are you baking? she asked every time she visited. No I am not, it's those damned dog biscuits. She hated that factory. They used to leave the gates ajar and kids used to walk across and try to jump the ravine – 9 feet it was on that side. Some people did used to throw themselves in of course and not for a good reason. Perhaps that's why they took the gates off the locks, to keep the water lower so it wasn't so deep. She grew up, married a man who worked offshore, moved to London… She'd been ill. She came home to Louth. Dad was aging. There were all the people she knew in the town. There was the canal – so many sides to it, the wildlife, the engineering – (She's more of an engineer than I am) – the barrel-shaped locks, the big old gate brackets, the water itself. It brought me on in leaps and bounds. Life isn't really that long in the end. You just get to know people and they're gone.

I left the rigs to work in London but I couldn't get work in London, ended up overseas most of the time. I thought why's she sitting there in that flat in London when she could be home. I worked off the coast twenty miles and more, that's why I know they should build all those windmills offshore, not bother about inland. There's wind offshore 365 days a year. They're finally realising. We could have told 'em, like we could have told 'em how bad diesel is for you. We used to joke we didn't have time for safety, but safety was what it all was – running all the systems, opening the wells, closing the wells, checking the pumps all the time, separating out the gas, the oil, the water – regulating 24 hours a day. We got on. You wouldn't get so much as a raised fist on the rigs – that man would be blackballed, not only from that platform, but from the whole of the North Sea. One summer we had a couple of osprey nesting up on the platform all summer. We used to stand on the handrails looking at the moon – the middle of the night stuff – you could get philosophical. He was working just North of Piper Alpha. He didn't stay much longer after that.

Keddington

It was a farm then in the '60s and all these gardens including the buildings was corn. I was a lorry driver, working like 'ecky to keep these going. I gave it up, thought I'd set up by myself and do anything I could to make a living. I knew if I had a chance I had to do gardens, set down trees years ago so they were established. I'm here for life. I've dug my own grave across the way and everything. Come and have a look. I've got three of these mobility scooters now. It's peaceful, nice in't it – you can hear the water in the lock. I decided I wanted my own estate – couldn't afford to buy one, so I'd make one, and that's what I've done. Set the avenue then I decided it wants a castle wall looking up, so I made one. I just carry on doing bits and bobs, can't do a lot but I do what I can. It occupies my mind and gets me about. I'm setting these stones for that statue there. I used to be an 'oarder, I used to think one day I shall use that, and I do – that's how the yard started. One of my lads he keeps that going now. Things is changed. I used to have seven lads working for me. He does it with three lads. One machine does away with two men now.

Ticklepenny

Up by the canal, even at night, moon and water cast some light. Little owls shriek. The nocturnal creatures see what we cannot. The lock keeper, Ticklepenny, warns that the ice is thinning but Ida and her brothers went on – she wasn't the type to listen to naysayers, or she'd never have got to London to train as a teacher. All that learning and wanting and knowing. Back home, time to let go a bit, out skating on the water in moonlight. Her brothers were rescued but those heavy skirts pulled her down – they just couldn't get to her. Even the new woman's skirts in 1909, they only just cleared the ground.

Alvingham

I got married and went to the farm. We found our own recreation really. When you're farming, there's always something going on. We had wheat, barley, oil seed rape – we used to breed Lincoln red cattle and we'd sheep as well. They used to come early Summer every year and dredge it out and all the debris they used to put it on the side, and the next year on the other side, for the farmers to deal with. They'd wait well into the Autumn and it dried out in the sun in the summer, then the men would burn it. The water used to run at such a speed when they got it dredged out. My mother-in-law married in 1912 and went to the farm. She remembered those barge boats that used to come up the canal with coal to Louth. They used to have those big round white ships biscuits – just flour, sugar and water really – and the men used to throw them to the kiddies on the bank – they used to line up for 'em, they loved 'em.

Austen Fen

Amaryllis means refresh, she thought – *that's what you should feel when you get home, refreshed.* The Victorians thought determination, especially in love, from the classic story perhaps, or the determination of a country girl, whose father worked for Claytons Coal Merchants, who married a man whose grandfather used to fetch the coal from the boat, who started in a caravan in a garden across from windswept Austen Fen, who made four children from nothing. Now he's gone from the tumour, she carries on, keeps her hands knitting and her kettles full – *no mains down here – all the water's pumped out – if we've no electric, we've no water.* Or perhaps Amaryllis, from Greek amarussein, sparkling like her mother after dad took all eight of us to chapel so she could take her bath in private in front of the fire, sparkling like the water when we used to pack a picnic on a summer day and take all the children down the canal. *They'll leave it as it is now won't they – after all, we've got the reservoir off it now?*

Irebeacon

The old pub, the Ship Inn used to be on the corner at Firebeacon opposite the warehouse
– then bad weather came and it fell in the canal. The family built their bungalow and
started making boats. This cow – she'd had a calf too young, it sends 'em a bit loopy.
They fetched her out the canal three times for the farmer. In the end he said *you can
have her. That was how we got into cows*. We kept the cattle safe, but we'd no more horses
after the neighbour's pony went in and died didn't it? Dad ran across the water pipe
with the lad on his shoulders, everyone on the bridge cheering. As boys, they tried to
bike it – they fell in. We didn't care, used to swim in it anyway, playing down there with
the dogs and everything – wouldn't now, all the chemicals off the fields, more than
there used to be. If only it could be put back into use – it would be brilliant, anything
that would bring activity here – pubs back on the side, rowing. Only folk come here
now is when it gets high, people come to gawp at it 'cause they think it's going to come
over. *Don't write that down.*

Tetney Lock

She was ten, going from place to place, school to school. She started fishing when she started knitting, at 4. Dad was in the navy. Grandad bought it in the pub for 3 grand, rang him up and said *I've bought you some land and water son*. Dad always wanted to be near water, to fish. They travelled across Germany, landed at Immingham around 1970. The grass was bigger than her, *but I was only a little diddy* watching the cattle being walked through the village along the canal to be grazed, tiddler-snatching with her dad after school on the pond or down Waithe Beck. They built the place from scratch themselves, springs everywhere you dig. That's what did for the old clay pits at the end of the nineteenth century, so it was all left as is till two dentist brothers started using it for fishing. They put the carp in but the rest just came, all the English coarse fish. We leave it natural now. The hawthorn that's bounding the property self-sets everywhere – left to themselves, trees do what they want, like the geese – and the weather moves things around.

Notes and Thanks

Images:
Cover image: Judith Tucker, *Excerpt from Tributaries*, (2013) charcoal, varnish and pigment 61 x 76 cm
Image on page 6 Judith Tucker, *Excerpt from Tributaries*, (2013) charcoal, varnish and pigment 61 x 76 cm
Image on page 33 Judith Tucker, *Only Birds Cross Over* (2014) charcoal, varnish and pigment 38 x 122 cm
Image on page 60-61 Judith Tucker, *Behind Land* (2014) charcoal, varnish and pigment 38 x 122 cm
Image on page 80-81 Judith Tucker, *Excerpt from Outfalls*, (2018) charcoal, varnish and pigment 61 x 76 cm
Image on page 108 Judith Tucker, *Excerpt from Outfalls*, (2017) charcoal, varnish and pigment 61 x 76 cm
Image on page 128 Judith Tucker, *Excerpt from Outfalls*, (2018) charcoal, varnish and pigment 61 x 76 cm

These poems were all written as part of collaborative place-based projects with the artist Judith Tucker. They emerge from what could be described as fieldwork, poetry based on walking through, and engaging with, place, with Judith, and, increasingly, with people who live in and visit the areas concerned. Some research into the areas concerned has also taken place and contributed to the work. Up until this moment, they have been pieces in flux. Shorter related poems or fragments have been exhibited with drawings and paintings and many of these longer pieces have been read at openings and poetry readings. Here they can be seen as a body of work. Although the earliest of these poems was originally written in 2011 and the latest in 2019, they have been edited and re-visited throughout the whole period, and indeed the places are also re-visited. *Tributaries* was part of a Holmfirth Arts Festival commission, 2011-2013. It focuses on a small triangle of moorland just beneath Black Hill in the Peak District. The Pennine Way forms the top of the triangle, below which many streams and becks flow down to the apex of Digley and Bilberry Reservoirs. The sides of this triangle can be seen as between two roads, the Greenhead Road to Manchester (A635) and the old lane, Issues Road, which peters out on to the moor. Thanks to Jonathan Best, Fiona Goh and Keith Griffin for their parts in commissioning this work.

The other projects represented here are all based in Northeast Lincolnshire. Humberston Beach and Creek and the Fitties Plotland are just down the coast from Cleethorpes. The poems then lead us along the flood bank walk from Humberston to Tetney Lock where we first discovered the outfall of the Louth Canal which runs on to Louth. Many thanks are due to all the people who gave freely of their lives and experience in conversations and interviews on the coast and along the canal. The Fitties Voices are all from conversations with inhabitants and visitors to the Fitties; they are all composed entirely of words spoken by individuals condensed and shaped into poems. *Louth Stories* incorporate found text from conversations with some linguistic re-shaping and fragments of original material.

Most of the poems presented here are small-scale localised walking poems covering walks of a few miles in different seasons. The titles of the *Tributaries* poems convey their locations. The *Humberston Beach and Creek* poems trace a repeated walk along the beach from the Fitties to the marsh and back. The

Humberston to Tetney Lock poems are written in response to a walk along a raised path between these two places, with three forays out onto the marsh at Tetney Haven. The poems here are also all seasonal poems, as their titles suggest, with the additional attempt to portray a sense of time of day in the beach poems where light and tide is so central to how we perceive sea.

The Lincolnshire work originally emerged from two commissions, both parts of larger group projects (*Excavations and Estuaries* and *Under East Wind*) curated by Linda Ingham – we thank her not only for engaging us in this work, for her consistent support, but most importantly for introducing us to this landscape. Thanks also to film-maker and artist, Annabel McCourt for her sensitive film of our work, and for a memorable summer playing/working together on the Fitties in 2016. In Louth, huge thanks are due to Paula Hunt and all the members of the Louth Navigation Trust who were so helpful in our Outfalls Project, introducing us to local people and hosting our work.

Thanks are due to the Arts Council and to Sheffield Hallam University for supporting this work. I should also like to thank Jo Dobson, Dan Eltringham, Veronica Fibisian, Andrew Jeffrey and Chris Jones for their support as part of the wider community of writers in Sheffield whose work engages with similar concerns – and in Andrew's and Jo's case, their help working with people on the Louth Canal in 2018.

Thanks to Tony Frazer, a most loyal editor, always calm in receipt of difficult manuscripts.

The greatest thanks of course go to Judith Tucker. All these poems are ours in a very real sense. The few drawings included here are indicative of this, and of a far larger body of work. If you'd like to see more of her drawing and painting in conversation with my texts, the following artists' books are related to the places considered here:

neverends: poems and paintings, with Judith Tucker, Wild Pansy Press, 2018 (The Fitties).

outfalls: poems and drawings, with Judith Tucker, Wild Pansy Press, 2018 (Louth Canal).

behind land: poems and paintings, with Judith Tucker, Wild Pansy Press, 2015 (Humberston coast).

sound unseen: poems and drawings, with Judith Tucker, Wild Pansy Press, 2013 (Tributaries).

We have also written about our work in a practice-based research context:

"Poetry, Painting and Change on the Edge of England", *Sociologia Ruralis*, 2019.

"Off path, counter path": contemporary collaborations in landscape, art and poetry" *Critical Survey*, 2017.

"Drawing closer": an ecocritical consideration of collaborative, cross-disciplinary practices of walking, writing, drawing and exhibiting (with Judith Tucker), *Extending Ecocriticism*, Peter Barry and William Welstead, eds, Manchester University Press, 2017.

Harriet Tarlo

www.ingramcontent.com/pod-product-compliance
Lightning Source LLC
Chambersburg PA
CBHW080447030726
47592CB00011B/3003